What Your Momma Never Knew About Men

A Guide to Creating Real-ationships

Latonya Black Gilliard

*Testosterone info from www.medicinenet.com

Copyright © 2016 Latonya Black Gilliard

All rights reserved. No part of this book may be reproduced or transmitted in any form or by any means, electronic or mechanical, including photocopying, recording, or by any information storage and retrieval system, without permission in writing from the publisher.

Published by Gilliard Media Group, Los Angeles

ISBN-13: 978-0-9983783-0-5

First edition

DEDICATION

This is dedicated to my mother, Hazel Black. No matter what you did or did not know, I know that you will always love me. Thank you for teaching me what unconditional love is.

CONTENTS

Dedication

Foreword

1	Why Does He Act That Way	5
2	What Masculine Men Need	12
3	Understanding Masculine and Feminine Energy	26
4	What You Should Look For in A Partner	41
5	Todays Pool of Men	50
6	Creating the Real-ationship	56
7	Tips and Nuggets	69

FOREWORD

by Carl Gilliard

On Saturday, December 28, 2013, much to my surprise and unbeknownst to me, my life would change forever. I was at a KWANZAA party in Los Angeles with a date. This was a party that I almost didn't attend because I was exhausted.

After intense procrastination, I decided to go. So I jumped into my car, raced to CARSON to pick up my date, then back to LOS ANGELES to this KWANZAA PARTY. The party had been going on for some time when we arrived. Upon arrival, we're standing in the center of the floor, when this gorgeous chocolate brown skinned woman approached us smiling. With her hand extended, she introduced herself.

"Hi. I'm your FACEBOOK FRIEND, Latonya Black."
I have 5000 "friends" on Facebook, so this happens frequently when I'm out. We did the friendly hug thing, I introduced my date to her and it was done... so I thought. It was a pleasant simple brief encounter; harmless even. As she walked away, I made note of

her beautiful legs and welcoming smile. When I returned home that night, I looked her up on FACEBOOK and sure enough, there she was!!! That was it...but I did "mark" her in my memory.

A few months later, after my relationship unexpectedly ended, I was sitting in front of my computer blowing off time. I look up and whom do I see? It's the dark and lovely Latonya Black with the nice legs I'd met some months earlier. I shot her a direct message. She responded. That first conversation lasted about two hours. Very flirty and fun. I wasn't exactly ready. I had gone through a crazy divorce, then was in another relationship; that one was very satisfying, but once it was done, I was ready to "do the dern single thing." That wasn't "to be." Latonya and I continued to see each other...all the time. The rest is history. We were married 8 months later on December 28, 2014; approximately one year to the date of that initial chance encounter.

I should also add that, because of my "financial situation" and given the circumstances surrounding my divorce, marrying Latonya was a "sho nuff" act of faith. (By the way, lots of dudes refuse to marry or date seriously when they "feel" that their money isn't "correct"). I'm glad that I didn't allow my past to unduly influence my future! Latonya is the best thing that has happened to me. Her influence on my life is immense and permanent. When you read this book, you'll understand why. Every word, contained in these pages, is true. She lives this. I live this. After I read "What Your Momma Never Knew About Men," I quipped, "So this is what you did to me?"

It's a joke, but absolutely true. SHE intensely understands the POWER IN HER FEMININITY. Latonya is confident, she's beautiful, she's lovely and she's truthful. There is no pretense in her or in this book. These thought provoking pages won't teach you how to "act" with the men in your life. They will help you connect with the woman you are; the woman God assigned you to be. If you're married, it will help your relationship improve 1000%. If you're single, you WILL attract the man WHO WILL APPRECIATE THE WOMAN YOU ARE.

God intended for us to complement each other and not to BUTT against one another. The true POWER in women lies within the marrow of her femininity. When she is FULL BLOWN and OPERATING in that, SHE WILL be happier and more fulfilled. The man in her life will be freer to OPERATE in his masculinity; which is Gods perfect design for him. We desperately need your help...not your condemnation. I've been there. But not with Latonya Gilliard. Latonya is an excellent wife, a true Proverbs 31 woman. She's my gift from God...and now you, the reader, will learn how you can be a blessing to those near and dear to you.

I can't wait for you to read "What My Momma Never Knew About Men", authored from the heart of my wife, Latonya Black Gilliard.

Enjoy!!!

Chapter 1

WHY DOES HE ACT THAT WAY?

He's a testosterone factory! It's that simple. Men have a need, as well as desire, to protect, lead, conquer, and provide. But do you understand how testosterone makes him function? Well, to begin, let's see how you understand their physical makeup.

DO YOU KNOW WHAT TESTOSTERONE IS?

This hormone gets us into lots of trouble sometimes!! I bet you never really thought about how important it is and how it affects a man's thinking. Let's go deeper!

*In humans and other mammals, testosterone is secreted primarily by the testicles of males and, to a lesser extent, the ovaries of females.

It is the primary male sex hormone. Testosterone is the most potent of the naturally occurring androgens. The androgens cause the development of male sex characteristics, such as a deep voice and a beard; they also strengthen muscle tone and bone mass.

DO YOU KNOW WHY MEN HAVE MORE TESTOSTERONE THAN WE DO?

Women don't have testes and prostates! We know that the testes/testicles is where sperm and testosterone are produced. Then, there is the prostate.

The prostate is a walnut-sized gland located between the bladder and the penis. The prostate is just in front of the rectum. The urethra runs through the center of the prostate, from the bladder to the penis, letting urine flow out of the body.

The prostate secretes fluid that nourishes and protects sperm. During ejaculation, the prostate squeezes this fluid into the urethra, and it's expelled with sperm as semen.

> **LADIES**: *If you find yourself dating a man aged 50 and older, you may find that he has inflammatory issues that require many bathroom breaks. You must be understanding of this, it's pretty normal for this age range.*

This helps you see why men are physically prone to being just who they are...masculine, bigger muscles, more physical strength, and domineering. I explained the prostate function because this is why men project and thrust to bring forth life, while we women receive.

When a man hasn't had sex for a while, he experiences a "pressure," a build up of this fluid, which must be released. This pressure can build up within a few hours, or a couple of days, after his last sexual encounter; it depends on the man. This is why men require sex more often than women.

When this pressure is present, his sexual desire is heightened and every woman looks like a lamb chop! Women walking down the street, women playing volleyball on the beach, women on the praise team or choir, teachers, every woman that has boobs and hips! His fantasies accelerate, even though he tries hard to turn his eyes away.

> **LADIES:** *This is why dressing modestly, in places where the attention should not be on you, is necessary. Though some of us will look sexy in a burlap sack, try to tone it down in church!*

Married men are not immune to this. Though they surely can't "touch," they will still look. Men are visual, receiving much satisfaction through their eyes. A woman's body is like a fine work of art and men sure do "appreciate" it.

It's not unusual for men to let this urge drive them into illicit affairs. In the Old Testament, it was unlawful for men to have sex outside of marriage. This is why they had several wives!

If the wife was pregnant or on her cycle and couldn't have sex, the other wife was usually available, or the next one, or the next one...you get the picture.

In these modern times, one wife is all a man can tolerate! Yes, polygamy is still allowed in spots, but is illegal in most of our country. Most women are not into sharing, so men must be extremely disciplined in order to turn down the myriad of women that are available.

A high level of testosterone makes it very difficult for men to by loyal to one woman. Heck, even when the level of testosterone lowers, as a man ages, he still may have trouble. This is when maturity and a strong desire to please God must be at his core. The struggle is real!

DO YOU UNDERSTAND MASCULINE ENERGY?

Masculine energy is drawn from masculine characteristics, the same way feminine energy is drawn from feminine characteristics.

We all have a mix of both energies. A very masculine man is what we call the Alpha Male. He is dominant, aggressive and knows who he is. He stands strong in his position and will fight for what is important to him.

> **LADIES**: *I am married to an Alpha male (yes, the fraternity and the noun). He requires a feminine woman or he will implode! He's a great leader and in my wisdom, I recognize his softer side comes as a result of me knowing how to let him be the man. If you have one, you will get the best results by being vulnerable. He'll be eating out of the palm of your hand; he just wants to please you!*

Masculine energy makes him take great pride in himself and he is to be respected and honored. Some men are able to draw from their feminine energy, which rounds them out a bit, softens the edges.

Masculine energy, characteristics, and behavior is observed by the female and used to determine whether there is an attraction. Too little masculine energy is considered a "nice guy," while an excess can be considered a "bad boy."

Men have been taught by other men, women, and society that this can be "good or bad," when it comes to attracting women. Sometimes it's hard to figure out which one he really is, especially when he's trying to conquer or impress.

If you like "bad boys," you must be aware that there may still be a high level of immaturity present, especially in younger men like this. They feel they have to be "over the top" in order to present this persona and most times, it covers up the fact that they don't really have their lives together yet and deep down, they feel inferior. In other words, bad boys can really be...bad little boys.

Men have bigger muscles, they are physically stronger than women, and their skeleton is more massive. These physiological differences are for a reason. Men were created to have dominion and rule. The more testosterone he has, the more dominant he is.

So, there you have it! This is why he acts the way he acts. This is why he feels the way he feels. I call it the Law of Testosterone. That law says, you cannot CHANGE a man when this hormone makes a stand! And this hormone will ALWAYS make a stand!

As a woman, you must know what kind of man you desire and what kind of man you have now, so you can adjust, compromise, accept or say goodbye

---

The Law of Testosterone

You cannot change a man when this hormone makes a stand...and this hormone will ALWAYS make a stand.

Chapter 2

WHAT ALL MASCULINE MEN NEED

Men are some of the simplest beings on the planet. When it comes to a woman, they only need 5(five) things from you:

- Respect
- Sex
- Sweetness/Kindness
- Feed Him
- Appreciation

That's it! Not necessarily in that order, but that's it. Why isn't love on the list? To a man, respect IS love.

YOU MUST KNOW HOW TO WALK IN YOUR FEMININE ENERGY in order to get the most and best out of a relationship with a masculine man!

ALL MASCULINE MEN NEED A FEMININE WOMAN.

I could really end the book right there!

It's all about balance...the Yin and Yang.

Let's go into some deeper details that your momma probably didn't understand or didn't know how to relate to, bless her heart.

RESPECT

At the very core of their being, men require respect. Respect, to a man, is honoring his authority, giving him the place of the "head" of a home or the allowing him to take the lead. Men fight for respect. They crave respect. It's in their DNA.

Much like two rams battling on a hillside, claiming their territory, men will fight to have what they want. If a man loves you and feels like you "belong" to him, he will fight to protect you and your honor. Look at all the films where someone has killed or hurt the girlfriend, wife, daughter, or friend, of a leading character *(probably written by men)*. He does whatever it takes to rescue the lady or kill the enemies. Yes, men are very territorial and that is the way they are created.

Today's man knows how women are all about equality and independence. When you start dating, they will play their need for respect down, for a little while, just to see what category to put you into. Either you are a toy or a keeper. The TOY is the woman that comes with demands and high-maintenance tendencies, with very little to offer him.

She strikes his curiosity for a little while but she doesn't respect his need for leading; she is quite masculine, even though she's pretty, outwardly. If the Toy doesn't realize that she falls into this category, she will truly get played. The KEEPER is quite special. She shows him RESPECT, let's him lead, inspires him, and her inner beauty makes her even more attractive. She's the one that gets to meet his inner circle.

> **LADIES:** *Now that you know this is a requirement, try it. If you want a serious relationship with a man, and you don't want him to be passive, give him the gift of RESPECT.*

Respect is what he craves, though it is not what every woman gives him.

How do you do give respect?

- Well, first, you allow him to be a man. If he wants to open your car door, carry the groceries, pull your chair out at the restaurant, walk on the street side of the sidewalk, LET HIM. This makes him feel valued and allows his need to protect you to be honored.
- Allow him to be wrong!

He has an ego that already beats him up when he misses the mark, he doesn't need you to roll your eyes, shift your neck, and give attitude.

> **LADIES:** *My husband is right about things a lot. When he's wrong and I was right, I don't say, "I told you so." He already knows that.*

Learn to just laugh inside and watch his next moves. It's harder for a man to acknowledge that you were right about something when his ego is bruised, so don't add fuel to the fire. Remember, being right is not always the loving position, so take the loving, high road.

- Let him see your fun, carefree side. If you can laugh at his corny jokes, see his point of view, and just "get" him, it builds trust and if he feels he can trust you, he will open up even more.
- Let him be himself! If he wants to spend some time alone, in his man cave, don't feel threatened by it. You both need space sometimes. If he likes to work on cars, dance, act, cook, just let him do what brings him joy. He was probably doing it before you entered his life, so, if you want him to be successful and fulfilled, join his world, don't try to change his world to fit into your concepts of what you think he should be.

Even if you are just beginning to date, show respect. This is the only way you will get to know the **REAL** man.

It will penetrate his shields. As much as we ladies have been fooled by men just wanting to make an easy score, ladies who use them for a meal, or string them along, then dump them, have fooled men. Yes, men have feelings too! Mr. Right is just as cautious as you are. If he feels that you respect him, you are on the path to really getting to know his heart. Pay attention!

FEED HIM

Yes, it's mostly true. The way to a man's heart is through his stomach. Let's break this down into a simpler view.

If a man see's that you can create a home, meaning create a lovely atmosphere for him to come home to, this endears him to you! If you can cook, keep your house fairly clean, keep a stock of his favorite things, and make an obvious effort to have a peaceful home, then he's yours!

We all know that food is comforting. Who wouldn't want a great, home cooked meal? Sure, sometimes you just want to go out to eat and be spoiled, which is always on the menu! The main point about knowing how to cook and keep a home is that the home is the headquarters, the hub, and the heart of the relationship. The place where you both come to rest has to rise to meet you. It has to have a free flow of clean, clear, loving energy. It takes more than food to do this; it takes the mind and heart of a woman that knows how to do all this with love and joy. So, if you desire to be married and have a loving home, or you cohabitate with your partner, you must know the importance of truly being the lady of the house.

Serving his plate is very special to a man. He may never demand it because he's used to dealing with women that have never offered it and plus, he can take care of himself. If you want to spoil him, and create that sparkle in his eye when he thinks of you, fix his plate! Yes, you may be laughing but this is so rare that it makes him feel special.

> **LADIES:** *Be warned! If you start this, he quickly gets spoiled and expects it. It makes him a big baby, but YOUR big baby! Be prepared to do it with love and not out of duty.*

This is one thing my momma knew about men! I can recall seeing my mother doing this for my father. I thought she was just over-doing it. My father had come to expect it; he never got up, except to get his own second helping, sometimes.

Once, my mother came to dinner at my home, during my marriage to my ex. She noticed that I did not fix his plate and asked why. My ex responded that he could fix his own plate. She never said anything more about it, never taught me the value of it.

Today, I realize that this is something that we aren't taught and honestly, it is one small thing that can really improve your relationship. Because men require respect, this one little thing can literally wrap him around your finger. It makes him think that you are super special and probably, irreplaceable. Women's liberation has taken away these small, invaluable acts of affection. This is so easy to do, especially if you love, adore and are proud of your man.

I can admit, I didn't feel valued and appreciated, in my past relationship, and I didn't feel like doing anything like this.

I felt that if I cooked, fixed plates for the kids, he could fix his own plate. Honestly, if you don't have a lot of respect for your man, and if you are not proud to tell everyone he's yours, you won't see the need or value in something like this. If you ever feel this way, there are some deep, serious things that you need to deal with in your relationship and fixing a plate won't help.

SEX

This one is easy. We already talked about all that testosterone that men have, coursing through their body like speeding bullets. If you ask any virile, healthy man what's important in their relationship, sex is always in the top 3. They must have it. They will do what it takes to get it. *I'm not talking about stalkers and rapists, that's someone else's book.* It makes them have bad judgment. Yes, if they don't get it at home, they may get it somewhere else. Does that make it right? Of course not!

Some men have the discipline and fortitude to stay faithful, no matter what. They are called Unicorns! Most men don't have that discipline. I have seen some long-term marriages that survive because they make sure they have sex at least 2 or 3 times a week.

For women, it's quality. For men, it's quantity. Sex is the highest form of physical intimacy two people in love can experience. It brings you closer together.

Sometimes, all that's needed is a snuggle on the couch, watching a movie. Depending on your man, that snuggle always ends...with sex.

This is physical release for a man. Pressure builds and causes all kinds of issues mentally and physically, if they don't have sex on a regular basis. In a relationship, women may turn sex down, but most men won't, even if they don't feel like it, which is rare.

Women often wonder, why do men cheat? Well, this is a huge part of the reason. The fact that he HAS to have sex surely doesn't make cheating right! It does, however, give you a bit of knowledge and a chance to use wisdom. It is rare, VERY rare, for a man to have the self-control and inner-calm that it takes for him to abstain from sex. Even men that are trying to abstain for religious, moral reasons have a very difficult time and a high percentage just can't do it.

If you know your husband/partner has a weakness in this area AND he does all that he can to honor and respect you, then it's only wise to help him out, even if you totally trust him not to look for sex elsewhere.

- ❖ Don't let him attend events alone, especially if women always surround him.
- ❖ Wives, have sex when you just don't feel like it. Sometimes, you just might change your mind, once you get started!

Even if you do all these things ladies, there will always be some woman out there with eyes for your man. Though he may do his best to avoid all situations of being alone with any woman, those moments are sometimes inevitable. Stand in your confidence and be observant. No need to read his text messages and emails. That will only make things worse AND show your desperation and lack of trust.

Have the conversation about other women and see how you feel about his responses. Only time will tell and his behavior will speak for itself.

If you ever find yourself getting jealous, you must relax and remind yourself that he chose you! You are beautiful, sexy and fabulous; he'd be crazy to step out on you!

SWEETNESS/KINDNESS

"You can always catch more flies with sugar than you can with vinegar." My mom still says that today! *(I used to clown by saying, "who wants to catch flies?")* Actually, this is true for everyone.

Show me someone that hates it when people are kind and nice. Hmm, maybe the Grinch? No, even his tiny heart grew when he recognized love. A man will choose a sweet, kind, smart, struggling waitress over a beautiful, financially successful, sharp tongued, masculine woman every time.

Be aware of your tendency to fuss and complain about the way he does things. If he's working hard to provide for you, he doesn't need to come home to a negative woman. Be willing to communicate what you feel in a peaceful, loving way. This will always get better results.

Most of us would love a masculine man that knows how to take charge, has his life together, treats you like a queen and makes you feel proud to be with him. **BE ADVISED**; this type of man works best with a very feminine woman.

A woman that knows how to make him feel like he's THE man, and she doesn't see this as a weakness.

If he trusts you with the private, sincere details of his heart, his weaknesses and hurts, he must really feel like you are his soft place to fall. It's actually the strength that every woman was born with, but has never been taught how to use it.

APPRECIATION

Men have hearts! When you show appreciation for anything your man does, he will be instantly gratified. Men have a deep need to protect and provide, so whenever they receive thanks for it, even though they were not asking for it, it expands his heart to do more, with a deeper feeling of love.

> **LADIES:** *Women's Liberation and feminist movements have basically perpetuated the forever "single" status of most successful women today. Mainly because they don't understand what masculine energy really is, and they have totally flipped feminine energy into something that it is NOT.*

When you show your appreciation, it must be true and from the heart. Most men have big egos that will expand to any kind of appreciation and recognition, so, if you do show appreciation and recognition, with an ulterior motive, you will soon get tired of doing it.

It's best to honestly observe his behavior and all the wonderful little things he does to make you feel safe, loved, honored and cherished. Sometimes, just saying thank you is enough. If he loves cake and he took a little more time to get some maintenance completed for your car, bake or buy him a cake! Do something special when he least expects it.

It doesn't take much to show appreciation. Sometimes, when a man does things that you think he should do anyway, you may not feel he deserves thanks. But always put yourself in another person's place. Your family may always expect you to cook and you do it graciously. But you can't deny how great it feels when they come hug you and say thank you for such a great meal.

Appreciation makes everyone feel better. Imagine how much better it makes your man feel, coming from you.

Chapter 3

UNDERSTANDING MASCULINE AND FEMININE ENERGY

We are all comprised of both masculine and feminine energy. Because of how we are raised and what we are taught, we may or may not strike a healthy balance of these energies within us. In romantic relationships, the balance of your and his energies must be like a delicate dance, or you will surely step on each other's toes.

Are you in tune with your feminine energy? Do you like to make things run smoothly and harmoniously? Are you at ease when your man takes the lead? Are you cool with letting someone think they have the last word? Do you prefer a man that treats you like a queen and adores you? Do you prefer your man to relax and let you spoil him sometimes? Do you prefer to dress in soft, sexy, feminine clothing?

If yes, you are probably more feminine than masculine and you are in touch with your intuition, letting it guide you in most areas of your life.

A feminine woman is at least 65% feminine and 35% masculine. This is not something I am referencing; this is totally my summation, based on myself.

I am probably 70% feminine, 30% masculine. I prefer my husband to do the heavy lifting, take care of me in a chivalrous way, meaning, open my car door, pull my chair out at the dinner table, pour my wine, take out the garbage, hold my hand when we are out, and walk on the street side of the sidewalk, as my protector. Yes, this may be a little old school but it's what I require. I can do all those things for myself but my husband does all this and it's what he likes to do.

> **LADIES:** *Being a feminine woman, I know how to speak my truth, with temperance and love, very effectively. I am NO pushover. We have had our share of serious, deep disagreements. We are two very strong personalities. The key to our success is this very yin and yang balance.*

My husband and I balance one another perfectly. He is definitely 70% masculine, 30% feminine. Again, he is an alpha male. He requires someone soft and kind, like me. He will never do well with a more masculine woman because they would bump heads all the time.

He wants to be in charge, he wants to be my provider and protector. No masculine man wants a woman with bigger balls than he has!

I prefer us to put our finances together, one account. This also means that we both trust one another explicitly. Many marriages crumble over finances, these days. With everything going into one account, he sees what I spend and I see what he spends. We have to communicate in order to make sure we stay on track. There is nothing to hide, we are a team.

It doesn't matter who makes more money, it's all OUR money. If we go out and he pays the bill, it's not from his account, it's OUR account.

We are always together in this area, nothing to hide. This is good for us, it works. You must do what works for you and your man, as long as you are not hiding anything and you both work well together.

Many women have been taught to have secret accounts, where you can put away money, just in case. Talk about planning to fail!

This makes you dishonest and it shows that you lack trust, amongst other issues. No masculine man would appreciate this. If he acts like he does, he's probably putting some money away somewhere too, making secret purchases. You both probably have had bad examples of this and you are going down that same, bumpy road.

Please know, a house divided against itself will not stand. Everything hidden is eventually exposed and you will have to deal with the mindset that makes you hide money.

If your mother did this, think about her relationships. Was she really happy? This is where we have to **UNLEARN** some of the dysfunctional lessons that were passed down to us.

Dishonesty never works in a relationship, especially a marriage.

ARE YOU MORE MASCULINE?

If you are a more masculine woman, let's say you are 70% masculine, 30% feminine; you prefer to be in control. This is ok, if you can find a man that is 70% feminine, 30% masculine. He will balance you out. He will be perfectly fine with staying at home with the kids, if you make more money.

> **LADIES:** *You still must see the treasure in this man and not take him for granted. Just because you are running things doesn't mean he isn't a man. As we said before, testosterone is still running through his veins. He may be in a situation where he is changing jobs, reinventing himself, or just changing his outlook in life but he still needs you to be a loving, kind wife.*

He will be the perfect Mr. Mom, taking care of the house and deferring some of the finances and big decisions to you. You must be totally great with this.

You must still be mommy (if applicable) and wifely, and you must still be kind.

Here is the clincher. I have seen these types of arrangements and relationships. They can actually work!

However, sometimes, the woman gets a little tired of feeling "in charge" and wants him to step up, be a little harder around the edges. What happened? Why did this balling, independent woman change like this?

The DIVINE FEMININE is what happened! Women are naturally nurturers. In today's culture, gender roles and energies tend to overlap.

As for women, no matter how masculine or controlling we are, there is a tender part of us that will come to the surface and want to be taken care of, if only for a little while! It is inevitable!

We must be in touch with this Divine Feminine part of us, the sacred wisdom that created worlds! Our feminine energy is powerful, even more powerful than masculine energy, for we birth life! The balance of the masculine and feminine is what is needed in today's world, to bring peace and harmony. Learn to allow the Divine Feminine to come forth, with all of her wisdom and strength.

What does the feminine woman look like?

- She's creative
- She enjoys making things work and assisting others, helping them be successful
- She's open and kind
- She's peaceful
- She is wise
- She is sensual
- She is compassionate
- She uses her keen intuition well
- She is sensitive
- She is approachable
- She is gentle in tone and manner
- She loves laughter and levity
- She sees beauty in all things

Know that being feminine is not being timid, whiney, weak, or helpless. Being feminine and knowing how to walk in your feminine energy is the most intelligent life a woman can live.

BEING INDEPENDENT

Today's independent woman tends to be more masculine. Yep, face it. It's not right or wrong, it just is. If you consider yourself independent because you feel anything less will cause you to lose your identity, you may need to re-think the term. Let's look at the Merriam-Webster Dictionary definition of INDEPENDENT:

1. Not dependent: as

a (1) : not subject to control by others : **self-governing** *(2)* : not affiliated with a larger controlling unit <*an independent bookstore*>

b (1) : not requiring or relying on something else : not contingent <*an independent conclusion*> *(2)* : not looking to others for one's opinions or for guidance in conduct *(3)* : not bound by or committed to a political party

c (1) : not requiring or relying on others (as for care or livelihood) <*independent of her parents*> *(2)* : being enough to free one from the necessity of working for a living <*a person of independent means*>

d **:** showing a desire for freedom <*an independent manner*>

(1) **:** not determined by or capable of being deduced or derived from or expressed in terms of members (as axioms or equations) of the set under consideration; *especially* **:** having linear **independence** <*an independent set of vectors*>

(2) **:** having the property that the joint probability (as of events or samples) or the joint probability density function (as of random variables) equals the product of the probabilities or probability density functions of separate occurrence

According to this definition, most women, fall into the category of being independent, even some married women. Do you think that being more feminine will make you less independent? I believe that this mantra has shipwrecked many women that desire relationships. Some of the most **misguided** thoughts about independence are:

1. I am financially independent, I have my own stuff, I don't need a man to take care of me.

2. Men claim they want a strong, independent woman, but when we show up, they run cause they can't handle a strong woman.
3. No man will ever be able to lead me; I'm too strong and independent for that.

Have you ever said any of these statements?

Well, if you find yourself proclaiming one of these mantras, how's that working for ya?

If you live by this and you still desire a mate or marriage, here is why you are probably still single:

1. A masculine, loving man, that wants a partner/to get married, will never seriously date/marry you because YOU DON'T NEED HIM!
   A MARRIAGE-MINDED MAN MUST BE NEEDED.

2. A masculine man, that wants a partner, will run from you because you are not feminine enough and he needs a feminine woman to bring out the best in him.
   YOUR BALLS ARE BIGGER THAN HIS!

3. A masculine man wants a genuinely sweet, nice, kind, tender woman (I didn't say pushover), and your more masculine ways will vibrate through even the most beautiful face and body.
YOU HAVE TO LEARN HOW TO BE VULNERABLE AND LET YOUR GUARD DOWN.

You can be masculine all you want, enjoy it, and own it! Just don't expect a marriage-minded man to sweep you off your feet.

Here are some traits of a masculine woman. **Not WRONG** traits, masculine traits. Yes, they are masculine traits, whether you consider them so or not. If you are honest enough to acknowledge that you embody one or more of these traits, you are on your way to wisdom, learning how to be softer and embrace your divine feminine.

What does the masculine woman look like?

- Treats those in service (waiters, valets, etc.) as low value help
- Is generally not kind

- Gives men advice like she's always correct
- Finds it hard to accept that she is wrong about anything
- Is unusually impatient
- Is very selfish, only concerned with her needs
- Tries to sabotage others when they disagree with her
- Is not very giving, except where it benefits her
- Gossips and justifies it
- Is uncaring
- Expects her man to follow her lead
- Is usually shallow
- Is slow to apologize, even when it's very clear she hurt someone
- Emasculates men
- Values wealth and image above love
- Prefers being right over being peaceful
- Sees being soft and vulnerable as weakness
- Expects a man to do everything while she offers very little

I could continue, but you get it now. It's very easy to disqualify yourself from these traits. No one wants to be considered as uncaring or shallow. If you are single, vocationally successful, and possess many "things," you must honestly ask yourself if any of these traits apply to you.

Typically, women have to embrace the masculine and fight in the corporate world to climb the ladder and get her equal share of the pie. Unfortunately, we sometimes don't know how to leave the masculine at the office, and it seeps into our romantic life, causing all kinds of turmoil.

There is a fine balance, yin and yang, that you must achieve in order to be your strongest, most empowered self. The healthy, genuinely feminine woman always finds more serious suitors than she can handle. Men are attracted to her like a magnet.

Do you desire marriage some day? Do you just want committed companionship, someone that cherishes you and makes you feel special? Are you willing to do the work on yourself and balance your energies? Or do you want to be single forever? Do you want to keep turning men away when they get serious? Do you want to keep penis swapping forever, never choosing one partner? Do you want to be a professional girlfriend? Do you want to keep dating until you are old and uninterested in men anymore? Do you deny wanting marriage because you have been hurt before?

At any given season, you will be asking yourself one or some of these questions. You owe it to yourself to honestly answer. A wise woman will recognize that her ideas of life will change; what she wanted last year may no longer be what she wants now. Allow yourself to graciously assess. It's not good for anyone to be alone, unless you feel called to it. If you are reading this book, you probably want a true love in your life. That's a good thing!

Examine your past relationship(s) and honestly admit to yourself what role you played in the ending of it. Now that you know how a woman can attract a man and most likely, keep him, set out to work on yourself!

Of course, there are some frogs, always will be. But now that you know more about how to handle and present yourself in a feminine way, you will have the upper hand in dating.

Let the goddess in you spring forth! This is the only way to really see what kind of man you have in front of you. If you let him be free to be the man, he will have no choice but to be himself and you will see exactly what kind of man you are dealing with.

Feminine energy is powerful. Please use your powers for good!

Men and women need not be at odds with one another. For if a woman would fully walk in her feminine power, we all win and there is peace.

Latonya Black Gilliard

Chapter 4

WHAT YOU SHOULD LOOK FOR IN A PARTNER

Everyone deserves a great relationship! As women, we all want to be happy, loved, cherished, adored, treated like a queen, spoiled, and needed. Guess what? Men want all this wonderful stuff too! MEN HAVE FEELINGS! You can't just treat a man any kind of way and expect him to just fall for you because you are beautiful, sexy, have a big butt, a lot of money, your own house, long hair, whatever physical trait you consider desirable.

If you want a partner, you must really KNOW yourself! You have to know what you require for yourself, in order to know what you can actually bring to a relationship.

Men look for certain qualities that attract them and even more qualities that keep them coming back to YOU.

A man that is playing the field is not horribly picky; he will take what he can get. But a man that is looking for a partner knows what he wants. He isn't going to throw his heart out there to just any woman that is attracted to him.

In order to know yourself, you have to be honest with who you see in the mirror.

- You must know if you are a morning person or a night owl.
- You must know if you like to cook or prefer to go out.
- You must know if you are a good listener or if you prefer to be running things.
- You must know if you want to be hunted or if you prefer to do the hunting.
- You must know if you love to shop and spend your well-earned money on shoes or if you want to spend more on creating a warm, inviting home.
- You must know if you can love a man that is in touch with his feminine side or if you do better with a take-charge man.

Do you know what your personality is like? Are you really able to see the truth, when you look in the mirror? If you put lipstick and a wig on a snake, a pig, or a butterfly, it's still a snake, a pig, or a butterfly.

That may be a bit harsh but you get what I am saying, right? You must know because you attract what you are! If you are a pig, you will attract a pig...but if you don't know you're a pig, then you will always blame the man and wonder why you keep attracting pigs!

You attract what you are, not what you want.

This is very important! Knowing these details about your own personality will save you a lot of heartbreak and wasted time.

It all comes down to your vibe, what makes you tick. We are all energy beings with vibrations that attract things, people, and events to us, just like a magnet.

Once you honestly answer yourself, it's time to get down to attracting the yang to your yin! Balance is the key. Yes, you should be your sweet, feminine self and you should also pay attention to his behavior.

****

These are just a few things to look for, in order to give you the best chance at having a loving, real-ationship:

KINDNESS/GENTLENESS

Any man that you attract must be TENDER, kind and gentle with you. Especially if he's an alpha male! You must only accept the kind of treatment that makes you feel safe and protected.

If he doesn't like something you did or said, is he controlling or does he kindly let you know his indifference? Is his smile genuine and inviting? Take your time and get to know his temperament. A mature man knows how to be tender with a woman. Accept nothing less!

ACCEPTANCE

What if the man of your dreams doesn't drink alcohol at all and you enjoy a cocktail or glass of wine sometimes? Is this a deal breaker?

Acceptance is mutual and you know that you cannot change a man. He must be able to accept you as you are, without trying to change you. He must accept your style of dress, your hair, your car, your intelligence, everything about you. Don't ever try to change to please a man, just be yourself. If he doesn't like something, it would be better for both of you to part ways and not offend.

If your own self-work demands a change, then, and only then, is it acceptable.

> **LADIES:** *I know a lady that smokes. Her boyfriend doesn't like it but he says he accepts it, as long as she tries to keep the smell away. One day, they were dressed up to go out and meet friends. They stopped at a store. When he went in, she stepped outside of the car for a smoke. When he came out, he yelled, "oh no, why are you smoking, you were so perfect!" This really offended her but it let her know exactly what he thought about her smoking. If he can't accept you as you are, then you must decide if it's a deal breaker or not.*

RELIGIOUS REQUIREMENTS

If you are a Baptist, and he's a Methodist, can you deal with that? If he's a Christian and you are a Buddhist, can he accept that? Some people that are "equally yoked" religiously are horrible together, outside of church. There are many couples with major religious differences that make them work because they can't see themselves living without each other.

If you close your mind because of differences, you may totally overlook your perfect partner. However, if you do find religious differences a deal breaker, make sure that is a spoken fact before you even begin dating. Sure, it would pay you to be more open-minded, but you have to be true to your beliefs.

MATURITY

Most men mature when they reach age 50, and some don't even mature in their 70's.

Most women mature much faster and that is a fact. This means you must be aware that men are on a constant journey to maturity. Sometimes, they remain like boys forever.

If you are a young woman in your 20's, still maturing yourself, your dating pool will be filled with immature men that think they know a lot more than they do. Some may not even know what it takes to be a man yet! Two people just beginning their life's journey can become a doomed couple or one that builds a bond that finds them sticking together like glue. It's rare but possible.

An emotionally mature man has an ability to communicate and handle pressure. He accepts responsibility for his life and shows the desire to move forward and grow.

If you have been dating someone for an extended period of time, and you desire the ultimate commitment, you must demand it or move on.

Do not blame him for not committing; blame yourself for not setting the tone for the relationship. It's totally in a man's nature to take what he can get. If you don't see your self-value, he will notice this. If you give your body to him, he will take it. Only the RARE man will refuse to take advantage of your weakness. Yes, there is a mature man that will turn you down sexually because he sees you are falling for him but he doesn't have the same feelings for you. Your feelings might be hurt but you should really be grateful for this unicorn!

HONESTY

It's great to have a man tell you up front what he is looking for in a partner. It's even better if his behavior matches his communication. Always be honest and clear about what you desire in a partner, too.

This is the best way to start any relationship but it truly works both ways.

RECIPROCATION

Let's say you have been in a relationship for a year, or more. You are totally committed to this man, hook, line and sinker, but you don't desire to get married. You may not live together but you take mini vacations together. You don't date other men. You spend quality time with your man and the two of you have confessed your love for one another. You have to admit to yourself, you have expectations!

When you are out, you expect him to introduce you as his girlfriend, lady, or sweetheart, not just his friend.

You don't require a minute-by-minute update when you are apart, but you expect him to at least check in with you, when he's out of town, the same way you do.

If you have a disagreement, you expect him to fight for the relationship to keep communication open, just like you do.

If he's not reciprocating, you must know that he does not feel the same way about you. He may say that he does, but his actions and behavior must match up.

Remember, YOU set the tone for your relationships.

Chapter 5

TODAY'S POOL OF MEN

(Slim Pickings)

Let's face it, there are so many types of men out here today, the dating game is sometimes depressing, stressful, and it seems you may never win.

Ladies, we have kissed many frogs, only to be disappointed that they didn't turn into a prince. As we get older, the pickings become less than slim. They become a needle in a haystack. Nevertheless, that one needle is worth going through the whole haystack because a *real-ationship* is always worth the effort.

So, let's take a look at all of the frogs that you thought could possibly turn into a prince but you are guaranteed to come away with a few warts first! Should you still kiss him? Use your intuition!

THE SMOOTH OPERATOR

He is honest enough to tell you up front that he does not want a serious relationship but will never come out and say that he is looking for a friend with benefits. He is very nice, comes to your rescue, when you need him, and he makes you feel like you are sexy and desirable. He goes on walks in the park, on the beach, and he gives great massages and even tells you his hopes and dreams. But don't expect him to commit! He is playing the field, enjoying his freedom, and if you start to get serious or want more from him, he slowly pulls away because you are no longer fun. What you see is what you get from him, don't expect more and don't get angry when he thinks you are crazy for expecting more. You should always believe a man when he tells you what he is!

THE EMOTIONAL ROLLERCOASTER

He is a great guy that has even mentioned that he wants to settle down but he needs some time. He needs to figure some things out because he's been hurt before and doesn't want to rush into anything. He takes you to the movies, dinner, you may even cook for him and spend some wonderful quality time...then he goes ghost. No calls, he won't return your calls or respond to your messages. You give up, frustrated and hurt, then, he calls.

His excuse, he has been keeping to himself, still needs time and you should understand. Well, this man is just full of it! You should run from him as fast as you can. If you want a committed relationship, honesty is important. He is either hiding something or just wants to keep stringing you along until some situation changes but he expects you to be understanding about the whole thing. If you believe his tales, you will be lonely, frustrated, and out in the cold. Get off this ride. Next!

MR. HIDE

He's the kind of guy that gives you hope. He is stable, likes to snuggle and watch movies, is totally into you but the conversations don't go deep, you don't really know the REAL him. You think you are exclusive but you notice that he doesn't really like to go out to big events, and he prefers to keep your relationship private and out of social media. You don't mind that, too much but when you ask him, he gets upset, even angry, and talks about how social media breaks up relationships.

With this guy, you really have to listen closely and hear what he's NOT saying. He lacks confidence. He's got some serious internal issues that you really need to explore before you get too involved. If he can't express his feelings for you, to your satisfaction, you may want to make him uncomfortable by inquiring. Whatever shows up, believe it!

MOMMA'S BOY

He respects his mother, calls her every day and treats her with such loving kindness that it impresses you. You think he must know how to treat women. Maybe he does. But does he know how to be a man and not just a son? These men have been well taken care of and sometimes, they don't know how to take care of themselves. Be extra observant of his living space, his spending habits and his ability to make moves and decisions without motherly input. You don't want to have to raise a man!

THE PRETENDER

He cares about you and it shows. You are totally convinced that he is your man and this is the real deal, after all, you had the talk. When you go out, you are happily on his arm and then, he introduces you by your first name only...not as his lady, his girlfriend, his baby, but only your name. Enough said. You need to have the talk again. He's probably more honest with his friends than with you.

THE EMOTIONAL MANIPULATOR

He's dangerous, even deadly. He worked his way into your heart, saying and doing all the right things. Then, slowly, he begins to criticize you, telling you the "little" things that you need to do to your appearance, building up your negative self-image.

He begins to compare you to other women, tells you constantly that you aren't doing enough for him, and says hurtful things that make you feel that no one else will want you.

He may not hit you physically but he tries to make you feel like you should be grateful that he has self-control. He may even try to keep you away from your friends and family, wanting you all to himself.

This isn't adoration! This is seriously wrong!

You may need help from someone, in order to leave, but you MUST LEAVE. This type of abuse frequently leads to physical abuse.

You surely deserve a king, not this damaged manipulator.

If this is your situation, please get help! Reach out to someone that cares or call the National Domestic Violence Hotline at 1-800-799-7233 (SAFE).

Chapter 6

CREATING THE REAL-ATIONSHIP

Now that you know what makes a man think and act the way he does, it's up to you to take this empowerment and use it to create the real-ationship that you desire. I combined those words because I know that you want something REAL!!!

In my introduction, I talked about how our moms taught us how to look for the bad things in boys, the things that we should stay away from. Things like:

- Boys just want to get in your pants, they don't want to be your friend
- If he doesn't have money, don't fool with him.
- No romance without finance
- Always have a secret account because he will probably end up leaving
- Men are no good, just dogs
- If he's too handsome, you will always have a problem with other women
- Men are a waste of time, build your career, you don't need a man

Well, some of us really listened! Some of us are still playing these tapes of our momma's voice in our heads today. We have to do the work of **unlearning** most of this implanted information, especially if it puts us on guard and keeps us from relating to the goodness of a man.

Of course, some of the stuff she said was right. Boys DO want to just get in your pants! And you should always look into the plans and goals that he has, before you consider joining your life to his.

To the contrary, I had lots of good "friends" that were male and they didn't try to get in my pants.

My best friend, for many years, was a male. I coached him through many relationships. I had the gift of being a great friend back then, too.

My momma didn't say all those negative things to me about money; it was never a factor when it came to my love life. Of course, it was the 80's and things weren't super expensive in the south. If he was cute, sweet, considerate, did all the things I thought he was supposed to do, like open my car door, pay for the date, treat me respectfully and have me home on time, he was a keeper!

There are many good men out there! Unfortunately, good is in the eye of the beholder. If your perception is skewed by bad information, you will always feel that there aren't any good ones left, they are all taken.

Let's turn things around! You can have a wonderful love life! The bad news is, it's all up to you. The good news is, it's all up to you! (Tweet)

Ladies, at any given time, in your life and growth, your wants and needs may pivot. You may just want to date. You may want to get married. You may want to be alone. Whatever your moment, you are in control. You have the power! There will be many men wanting to weave their way into your heart and/or your bed. YOU have the power to determine where any man lands in your life.

We must learn to trust our intuition. Our passion and desires tend to have urgency, a push. That strong need you have to find a man, or get married, have a baby... all so urgent! Our intuition, divine guidance, is calm, deep, solid but gentle. That is why I was able to override it easily and follow the urgency. It was usually the path to a hard lesson in love. But I learned and kept it moving.

Long-term Relationships

Many of you have been with someone for years. It's been ok, ups and downs. But when you feel you want more, trust the feeling. You are evolving. When the relationship begins to grow toward marriage, be patient and follow his lead but have the conversation! Ask the important questions. Let him know that marriage is what you desire. Although it's best to let him know what you desire and not let him string you along, letting him lead you into the marriage is designed to solidify his commitment. After all, if he wants to provide for you, protect you, be your biggest fan and make you his queen, he will go after you with all his might.

Why Is He Stalling?

Men have many reasons why they may be holding out on asking you to marry them. If everything is perfect, in his mind, he will pop the question, no hesitation.

But there are a few things that may make him hesitate:

- His finances may not be where he wants them to be yet. If a man feels he cannot adequately provide and give you the things you desire, he will plan, work, hustle, and save until he gets there. You may have a good job and just want to get married, but in his mind, things have to be perfect. You must allow him this and maybe, come up with solutions that he can agree with.
- He may love you dearly but there may be something about you that makes him question a marriage to you. It may be your attitude, the way you treat others, the way his family feels about you, something that makes him doubtful. Whatever it is, you deserve his honesty. Have the conversation!
- He's just not ready! Believe it or not, men really value their freedom and though they don't want to lose you, they may not be ready to lose their freedom. You definitely don't want to marry anyone thinking this way! Have the conversation!

Remember, you cannot control or mother him. At this point, continue to be kind, sweet, inspirational, supportive, and loving. Observe his behavior. The "representative" will slowly evolve into the real "him." If you sense anything in your gut, your intuition, that tells you to slow down or back up, PAY ATTENTION. It's at this point that we get warnings from our God-self about anything that we may be missing and just because we have gone this far, we tend to override the voice.

Like I said before, I have ignored that voice a couple of times and wish I hadn't. That is the still, small voice of God that always guides us. Why do we not listen? There are many reasons but remember, THAT VOICE IS USUALLY FIRST AND USUALLY RIGHT!

If things progress, great! You are heading in the direction that you desire and you both should be excited, even if you have been together for a long time. You should still be excited when you think of him. You two have a purpose for being together. There is a common goal. You both agree on the direction you will be taking as husband and wife. You can talk about anything and any disagreement only brings you closer, learning more about one another.

Insight for Wives

Your life is full of purpose and as a wife; you have added another element to the path of your life. You are not alone anymore. You are joined to your husband and the two of you should function as a team. Teams work together for a common goal...to win! Win in your marriage.

As a wife, you must learn to be the scientist of your household. Why do I say scientist? Because, as the queen of the house, you will:

- **Develop theories** – you will study and recognize that if you push certain buttons that you husband will react in a way that is not peaceful, so you wisely avoid unnecessary drama.
- **Create scenarios** – you will learn how to paint a visual or mental picture that will inspire your husband to continue to do what is best for his career, thereby, becoming his loving muse.

- **Conduct experiments** – you will try lingerie and different things to keep the fire burning and the embers hot...remembering that he is very visual!
- **Investigate** – looking into ways that you can assist your husband by keeping a peaceful, loving home for him to joyously return to every day.
- **Submit data** – you will "lovingly" submit to your husband. We need not fear the word "submit." As my dear friend, Relationship Expert, Ryeal Simms, instructs. *"We need your help, we need you to **submit your intelligence** to us! Not for you to feel inferior, but to see things that we don't see."*

So you see, being a wife is not to be entered into lightly. It's a huge responsibility! You must know how to be the goddess; the one that prays and creates, while letting your husband think and feel that all the great things happening was his idea! Feminine energy is stronger than masculine energy, so, you are not tricking him in any way. You are walking in the energy that created and birthed life!

Your strength is in your tenderness, your gentle demeanor. You may have to be tough in the corporate world but you must always know that your husband is not your employer and you are not his boss.

Wifely Wisdom

As a wife, you must understand that your need to be right has no place in your marriage. A wise woman knows that "losing" an argument is the only way to win.

As a wife, you must consistently pray that your husband be blessed to take care of you the way that he desires. Money, or the seeming lack thereof, can never become an issue that threatens the fabric of your team. For if the team is going to win, it cannot be you against him. A house divided will never stand and that is not what you promised one another, in your vows! Put your heads together and come up with solutions!

As a wife, you must continue to press toward the calling for your life. If you chose well, your husband will totally support you because he loves you and wants you to be happy. There is a plan for your life and it doesn't end because you got married.

As a wife, you must trust your husband even more than you did when he was your boyfriend. Demanding passwords should not be necessary.

Faith

If you are Believers, then you know that you must pray TOGETHER! Coming from a Christian perspective, the husband covers the wife and family, but he is not alone in this. As a Proverbs 31 wife, you are a helpmate, a lover, a friend, and a blessing to your husband.

You two are Spiritual Partners! The two of you, bound together by the power of prayer and your faith, are not easily broken. If you say that you love and support your husband, it cannot be by just words, your life and behavior must show it.

Our husbands can be very linear, thinking in straight lines, wanting to fix things, not so much looking at the softer, nurturing side of an issue, the way we do. Wives must use all of their God given intuition to see the invisible, expect the impossible, feel the intangible and pull that which your family needs into the present NOW.

Boaz was a powerful man. Ruth was a hustler, getting the job done, much like a single mom does today. He found her. He observed her. He was gentle with Ruth. He saw her heart and wanted to take care of her. Ruth was wise, caring, working hard to take care of Naomi. She wasn't looking for a man.

Naomi, however, knew about men! She schooled Ruth on what to do to win his favor. She told her how to prepare herself, observe him, and lie down at his feet. This may seem to be a bit forward but it was STRATEGIC.

Naomi knew that being at his feet would mean that she was submitting herself, all the while, appealing to his masculinity.

Now, can you imagine Ruth wanting to stand up to him and be a "strong woman," trying to tell Boaz what to do? She surely would have been left out in the cold. Women always want to be found by their Boaz, but they don't want to become the Ruth that attracts him.

Men haven't changed much. They are still bound to their testosterone, their DNA is still created to lead, provide, and protect. Actually, that is when they are at their best. Not wanting a woman to be docile, but to just let them BE A MAN. Except, today, men must know how to navigate the ever-changing personality of the masculine woman that has been programmed and liberated. Is she really free? Or has she created a world of uncertainty and dishonesty.

WE MUST ALLOW MEN TO GET BACK INTO POSITION!

If men were created first and given complete dominion over everything, what makes us think that this has changed? When he knows his purpose and why he's here, he continues to walk in dominion, until a woman, who doesn't know that she was originally placed here to rule beside him, tries to take over and tell him what to do.

Men want to please us, so, like Adam, they acquiesce, they bend, sometimes until they are no longer leading and hating every minute that they stepped out of their position. This goes against everything in their DNA and sometimes, they just don't know how to handle it or us. They are out of order!

The world has not functioned the way it was intended because of misplaced energies. It is going to take the wise, feminine energy to **realign** itself and force the masculine back into place.

Ladies, I am telling you what's on the test AND giving you the answers! All men are not equal in behavior, we know this. We have had our share of knuckleheads and boys.

When you encounter a REAL man, you will know the difference. Your response should be to let him BE a man. Get to know him. Don't fight him. Seek to understand him. If you are not interested, be lovingly clear about it. If you still like him, show interest and let HIM pursue you! If YOU do the pursuing, you take away his need to chase and put him in a position of following. That sets a precedent that may not be favorable in a committed relationship.

If you have been hurt before, BE WILLING TO BE HURT AGAIN. Feel the fear but love hard anyway! You will be just fine.

Balance with him. It's such a beautiful dance!

Chapter 7

TIPS AND NUGGETS

- ❖ WILLINGLY having sex with a man that is not in love with you and committed to you is like putting in a nasty tampon! It fulfills the purpose, at the time, all the while releasing toxins and poisoning your soul.
- ❖ A man that regards women highly will treat her like a lady, kindly, with respect. If these characteristics are absent, walk away.
- ❖ If you really love your man, and you would like him to make more money; don't emasculate him, inspire him and encourage him with gentle behavior, loving support and offer solutions. He already feels bad enough.
- ❖ Know that, if you make your man feel bad about earning less, you are slowly killing him with cancer…literally.
- ❖ Ladies, as much as he chooses you, it's YOU that has the final say. Choose wisely and love deeply.
- ❖ Women have a keen intuition. Always listen and question yourself, if you don't understand

what you are feeling. Help is always available, just ask!

- ❖ If a sweet, caring man tells you he only wants to have fun, hang out and fool around, BELIEVE HIM!
- ❖ Choose a man that you can easily respect, admire, and be proud to call him your man.
- ❖ Been hurt? Divorced? Jump back into the game and risk being hurt again! It's the only way to be successful at love and life.
- ❖ Some men mature later in life but there is always an exception to the rule. Never think that he will grow up "eventually." You just may be waiting for a long, long time.
- ❖ CAUTION: It is a great thing to pursue your dream and vocation. Just know that if this pursuit makes you feel like you don't have time for the relationship, marriage, and/or children you want, you may wait until it's much harder to have either. Many women, in their 40's and older, find themselves in a great career and single, desiring to be married and have children. By this time, the pool of marriage-minded men is much smaller. Prioritize and

balance your life with career, you actually CAN have it all!

- Before you look for a man to fulfill you, make sure you are happy with yourself! Fulfillment comes from doing work that satisfies your soul.
- You CANNOT change a man. You CANNOT change a man! You CANNOT change a man!
- A man changes his behavior for his own reasons. If he seems to change because of your urgings or threats, it's only temporary. You must accept him as he is or leave him alone.
- If you feel stressed, tired, alone, worn-out, trying to hold a relationship together, it's probably one-sided and he's not that into you. Move on!
- If you are content to have sex with a man BEFORE a commitment, KNOW that you are taking a chance that this will be the last time you see him! Blame yourself only!
- Work on your self-esteem. Learn to love yourself so much that nothing and no one can drag you into desperation and self-doubt. You are a queen, with or without a king!

- Seek first the call and purpose that God has for your life. Everything else will fall into place around it, even attracting your king.
- Don't be surprised if men seem to pay more attention to you when you think you look your worst, in a cap, sweats and sneakers. Real, mature men can see past the makeup, hairstyles and high heels. You are more relaxed, which makes you more approachable, more authentic. Try to stay that way, even when you are dressed up!
- Do the work, become the woman YOU love looking at in the mirror.
- Always think loving thoughts about yourself. The man you attract will do the same!
- Think for yourself. Following advice from women that are miserable will guarantee your miserable life.
- Master flowing in your feminine energy and power. You will discover a new life, full of joy and peace.
- If you know that giving him praise always raises his spirits, do it!

- ❖ If you notice any habits that are unhealthy, make subtle suggestions to encourage a shift in his behavior. Use lots of kindness.
- ❖ Before he finds you, know your purpose and be a whole, happy woman first. THEN, you will attract from your wholeness, not from desperation.
- ❖ As my husband says, "the Bible says to be not unequally yoked with unbelievers. But you can also be unequally yoked with someone who doesn't believe in you!"
- ❖ Walk in your feminine power at all times!

****

Ladies, we are strong, we are resilient, and we are emotional. Sometimes, those emotions take us to places that a man just doesn't understand. You must learn how to communicate what you are feeling in a way that keeps you connected to your integrity while engaging his heart. This is truly a skill that most of our momma's didn't possess.

So, now you know what your momma never knew about men. She did her best. As for you, use this information to develop the skill to create positive, healthy outcomes. Practice this wisdom and watch your relationships blossom!

Ladies, we can have it all! Health, love, prosperity, fulfillment, peace and joy! Share this wealth of knowledge with the next generation.

When you see me in a seminar or workshop, come up to me and tell me, **"Sistar, now I know."**

Peace and blessings!

ACKNOWLEDGEMENTS

Knowing that I am forever connected, plugged in and led by God is the only thing I can contribute my life to. I am eternally grateful for the gift of my Savior, Jesus, The Christ.

Carl Gilliard, my partner, friend, my love, my husband, I thank you for being the man that I need you to be. We are a team like no other. I couldn't do this without you. There is so much more I can say!

To my mother, Hazel Black, you are the love mold from which I was shaped. I simply adore you.

To my children, I will always be there for you, no matter what. You have gone through the thick and thin with me and cherish you with all my heart.

To all of my friends and family, all my Sistars, thank you for your continued support and prayers. I need you!

To all those that rubbed me the wrong way, thank you for helping me become polished, so now, I shine!

ABOUT THE AUTHOR

Latonya Black Gilliard is a southern born gem that has been on a perpetual journey of self-discovery. She is a singer, actress, author, transformational speaker, life coach, director and producer.

You can reach her at:

gilliardmedia@gmail.com,
Facebook.com/Latonyasings;
/LimitlesslifeCoachingandmentoring;
/chicksnnuggets; and Twitter/chococroon

Available for workshops, retreats, conferences, seminars, and corporate events.

Ask about the **Limitless Life Teen Summit**, an interactive workshop for today's youth, utilizing music and drama to educate, inspire and enlighten.

For bookings, contact Gilliard Media Group at:

(424) 243-6750

www.gilliardmedia.tv

What Your Momma Never Knew About Men

Connect with Carl and Latonya Gilliard on Facebook in the inspirational Facebook group, Built to Last; on YouTube/Conversations with Carl and Latonya

©2016

Gilliard Media Group

www.ingramcontent.com/pod-product-compliance
Lightning Source LLC
Chambersburg PA
CBHW070059100426
42743CB00012B/2593